Politics of Feminisms

Marla J. Selvidge

CONTENTS

Preface

Long ago, in the late twentieth century, when I was only seventeen, I began to study the Hebrew/Old Testament and New Testament while in college. I had this unshakeable faith that a Divine Being would never create inequality among human beings. There were passages in the Bible that confirmed my belief. People were created equal in Genesis one, and stood side by side in the formative years of the early church. Surely, after reading the Genesis passage and many stories in the New Testament, people would agree that females and males should be treated equally in society.

I was naive. Having been raised in a family with a strong mother who stood beside her husband as an equal, I could not even fathom that females should be treated differently just because their biology differed with males. I soon learned that females and males were treated differently in society. Even in my undergraduate college, I was suspended for wearing my skirts too short. I was told to lower the hems. Defiantly, I told them that the hems were already lowered. Did they want to purchase new clothing for me? My suspension was reduced from a week to three days and I was prohibited from attending classes. This decision caused all of my grades to be lowered ten percent because of an attendance rule. There were no such rules for males.

Packing several years of studying koine Greek under my belt, I headed for graduate school. In every class and in every paper I asked questions about females. I produced *Luke the Feminist* as crowning achievement of my Master's Degree. Faculty voted it as the best thesis of the year. During those years, there were no other feminists (that I was aware of) within hundreds of miles of my university. I found support for this belief in the equality of males and females by reading books by scholars from around the world.

Tackling my first job teaching in college was a nightmare experience. I wore long skirts to class, and began the task of attempting to help students learn to think critically. Students voted me as the Teacher of the Year, but faculty never heard a word I said in committees. I was alone in a man's institution. I left the job and hoped for something easier to do in life.

After years in other non-academic jobs, I hungered for intellectual conversation and something to challenge my brain. (I did not satisfy that hunger often, even in the academy.) Working in business positions such as a Personnel Director (Human Resources) was too easy and boring for me. I went back to college and was accepted into a male institution that had recently gone co-ed, Saint Louis University.

I don't have evidence that I was the first female accepted into the Ph.D. program in Biblical Languages and Literature, but I think was. I remember only one other female in the program whose application was approved after mine. Some day I will write about the battles, inequality, the stealing of my work, and finally, the choice to go outside the university to find a dissertation director. These battles were the most difficult times in my life. At one point, I thought I would just leave the Ph.D. program and work for a restaurant. But I stayed.

I was researching how the writer of the Gospel of Mark treated females. The Jesuits made fun of me. "There are no tulips in Mark." Every time I would hand in a chapter, my dissertation director would hand back thirty pages of corrections and challenges to prove my thesis. This went on for months. Finally, I realized that my dissertation director, and head of the program in which I was enrolled, was not going to allow me to graduate. I appealed to the Graduate Dean and asked for someone outside the university to be my director. It was approved.

Frederick William Danker, Ph.D. came to my rescue. I had enrolled in some of his classes and he allowed me the freedom to write about whatever I discovered. Among the things he taught me was to soften my language about females in the Gospel of Mark. He wanted me to be less authoritative and more congenial in my writing. I was not to be so smart. He came up with the title of my dissertation that masked its revolutionary views at the time, *Woman, Cult, and Miracle Recital*. After my oral exam over the dissertation, he said something like this to me, "I would do that again with you at the helm any time." I will chronicle these challenging times in a memoir soon.

But, as I look back on my Jesuit days, I realized that I was being prepared for the biggest challenge of my life, becoming a female professor in a field that had only a few females at the time. A poster of Princess Leia of Star Wars holding a blaster gun was plastered on my door. She stood watch over me. Without the battles with the Jesuits, I don't believe that I could have sustained a career in the academy. As the first woman in several institutions, learning how to survive and be successful at the same time became a daily grind. Colleges and universities no longer had rules about clothing but they still encased females in barbed wire to control them. The political, social, psychological, and personal strategies they used to control females left all of us abused and often disoriented.

Winning an academic job is one thing, keeping it is another thing. I began to give papers and write articles like a mad woman. Most of my earlier articles were published in foreign periodicals because American academic journals would not accept my work. Sometimes I submitted publications with my initials only. The Journal of Biblical Literature accepted one of my articles and made me rewrite it. It went to about five pages and twenty pages of footnotes instead of its twenty something original. It was a hoop I jumped through only once.

It was at one of the National Meetings of the American Academy of Religion or the Society of Biblical Literature, that someone said that my work was steeped in "feminist biblical interpretation." I had never used those words to explain my work. I thought I was just on a journey to find and explain texts about females within the Bible and in history. So, from 1980 until the present, my work has been labeled "feminist biblical interpretation."

Having published many books, probably the one that has been quoted the most is, *Notorious Voices. The Roots of Feminist Biblical Interpretation* (Continuum, 1996). My point here is not to laud myself, but to argue that I have been dead square in the middle of the development of feminist biblical interpretation for forty-five years. My conclusions at the end of my academic career about this quest are very different than when I started the journey so long ago. I am no longer a novice or naive.

This collage contains three articles. The first article was published online, "Feminism and the Future of Classroom Politics." It is one thing to be a starving female living on the edge of society and trying to make a living while teaching on the college level. It is another matter to be a woman who is a full professor, having published many books and created scores of college classes. The words of early feminists did not ring true in my classrooms with males coming from families living on the edge of poverty who were themselves sidelined. While they were certainly an "other" gender, they were not my oppressors. In a way, I was a "matriarch" in their college space. The voices of historic feminism had to change their strategies in my classrooms.

The second article is an unusual one. And those who have not read the documents might miss some of the nuances I make. The title is daunting, "Menses, *De Secretis Mulierum (Secrets of Women)*, and *The Dead Sea Scrolls.* A Comparative and Theoretical Analysis." I have shortened it to, "Misogynist Politics for a Thousand Years." A request came from an editor of a Catholic publishing company in Belgium to write about the miracle story of the woman with the flow of blood. She had read my dissertation and was thrilled with my analysis. Could I write something for her for a special volume of collected articles on the miracle story? The texts were to be selected from the middle Ages.

The Secrets of Women is a fascinating "medical" document about females. As I studied the document and its interpreters, I heard the voices of the men who wrote similar passages in the *Dead Sea Scrolls*, more than a thousand years prior to *The Secrets of Women*.

The similarities in the documents are astounding. My analysis and conclusions may challenge the reader to think about how we view texts about females in history. Thinking the article was published in the editor's collection, I found out later that it had been left out. They never bothered to contact me. The third article was produced at the request of an editor of an encyclopedia on "feminist biblical interpretation." I spent one year, or more, re-reading many of the books and articles that had crossed my desk during my long career. I produced this piece, only to have the editor tell me that it was "too difficult" for their readers. I suspect that her decision was political. It is one thing to be a dyed-in-the-wool feminist. It is another to criticize the methods and beliefs of feminism. In a similar fashion to fundamentalists of every persuasion, a hardline feminist does not want to hear any criticism of her beliefs or activities.

The photos of totems were taken (by the author) at Totem Bight Historical Park and Saxman Native Village in Ketchikan, Alaska. Why not include a little art with your written work?

Introduction

Why do people want to study the Bible? This might seem to be a silly question but it is not! Millions of people study the Bible for millions of reasons. The Bible is a book that belongs to the world and people from many walks of life and cultures study its contents. People consult the Bible for many of the same reasons that they choose to be religious. For many of them, it answers questions about the origins, responsibilities, and destinies of human beings.

Some people look to the Bible for a code or standard of morals in their lives. Others hope to find a single point of view or a single way of interpreting the Bible. Some want security and look for a structure that will support them psychologically and socially. Others want to know that a Higher Power is in control of them and their lives. They believe that the Divine created the biblical documents. For instance, dispensationalism systematically divided the Bible into "historical" epochs so that one could view a wide swath of the past and the future. There was no open-ended fuzziness about what was ahead. As a child, I remember a dedicated church member rolling out a twenty foot-long dispensational chart on the floor and walking me through it, all the while explaining that this was a map of my destiny. And there are those who continue to believe that the Bible is predictive, and read its pages to find signs of future events.

Life is not always predictable or controllable, and many look to the Bible for an escape from current circumstances. Some want to perfect themselves and those around them while creating a perfect standard by which to live. Others read the Bible for comfort, conversation, and community. They love its familiar pages. Some find companionship in its pages. Kathryn Kuhlman, the great Pentecostal faith healer believed that she had found a Divine lover in the Bible.

Others relish the history and the people in and behind the biblical documents; academically minded people enjoy systematizing important concepts into teachable precepts. Socially minded people find a call to help others, even to facilitate liberation for them from their dismal circumstances through violent means. Revolution, expansion, war, violence, and change are themes that dot the pages of the Bible from the beginning to the end. There is virtually no end to the reasons that people read and study the Bible.

Section One
Feminism and the Future of Classroom Politics

The New Testament, historically, has been foundational in constructing the identities, rituals, ethics, and beliefs of its readers. Its origins are pluralistic and international. Centuries of peoples have searched its pages to find meaning for their lives, their families, and their countries. It has spawned rituals for birth, death, and marriage. Many place the Bible at the center of their daily activities, trying to adapt their lives to its moral guidelines. They use interpretations of the New Testament to enlighten difficult ethical dilemmas, but there are others who use the Bible as a tool to enhance their own power over others. Monarchs, popes, politicians, and ecclesiastical authorities, as well as unlikely political alliances, have governed people in the name of the God of the Bible. Yet in spite of this theocratic dominance throughout the history of the world, there were dissenters who sought to promulgate or discover their own interpretations. This rich and diverse tapestry should be center stage when we open the pages of the Bible for our students.

Conversations with the Academy

My career has entertained not only conversations with many feminist scholars in the academy but it has also turned to the works of scholars that have been marginalized. As early as 1981, I thought that the typical academic discussion about the documents was too narrow. I found that I had to work overtime identifying primary sources to be used in the classroom that demonstrated pluralism and relevance to the cultures and peoples of the world.

Two of the papers I was privileged to read at the National American Academy of Religion and the Society of Biblical Literature in the mid 1980's urged listeners to broaden their perspective of the documents. At the AAR in 1985 and 1986 we discussed "Teaching New Testament in the Twentieth Century," and "Surface Exploration, Stratigraphy, and Digging up the Future." I encouraged listeners to add readings and assignments for from the Bacchae, Eleusinian Mystery Religions, The Book of Enoch, Hymns from the Goddesses, and other non-Christian and Jewish Apocryphal literature, and more.

Hoping to make the case for relevancy I suggested using newspaper articles as case studies on current topics whose historic basis was found in the Bible, especially developing countries. I pointed participants in the direction of assignments where students interviewed people from multiple denominations about their faith. I gave examples of how I used archaeology and art to interpret and explain biblical passages. And how I allowed my students to interpret a passage of the New Testament through any creative means. They used art, created music, videos, poetry, puppet shows, and more. Not only was I helping students to appreciate the cultural diversity of the first century, they began to recognize that the documents contained violence, racism, sexism, and more. The consensus at the end of these papers by academics who heard them, was that I was asking too much of them. They could not use the tools or the ideas because there was not enough time.

My scholarship throughout the 20th century investigated the abusive language that I detected in the New Testament. I studied violent language in the gospels and came to the conclusion that Luke-Acts was an etiological legend that legitimized violence as a way of conquering the non-Christian world. I recognized this same attitude of religious superiority in many of my colleagues, and argued with my sisters who were working on feminist articles that they were falling into the same trap.

Faint Voices from the Edge

For several decades within the academy faint voices have raised the issue of a multiplicity of interpretations, audiences, methods, and teaching the New Testament. In the first edition of my textbook, *The New Testament: A Timeless Book for All Peoples*, I attempted to address the purposeful neglect of international scholarship by developers of New Testament textbooks. Each chapter considered non-traditional approaches to studying the documents under the headings of Ethical Issues, Interpretative Focus, and Global Interpretation.

I included views from people of varying shades of color, Eco-feminism, Native American Interpretation, readings from the Quran, and reflections upon people who have embodied their beliefs, such as Dorothy Day. It focused upon people who synthesize their religious traditions such as Hindu-Christian, Same Sex Partners, Promise Keepers, and Latin American views of James. It included excerpts from the Cotton Patch Version of the texts, and the issues of alienation, violence, and pornography, to name only a few. Professors did not like this approach to studying the New Testament. They especially did not like the geographical organization of the text. I tried to group the literatures together from different parts of the ancient world. The second edition was reorganized in a more traditional way, but the emphasis on pluralism and internationalism and geography was thrown to the wind.

Historical-Critical Trap

The dominant methodological strategies used by most biblical scholars have consistently failed, in my view, to address the multiplicity and diversity of the origins, meaning, relevance, and development of the texts. Many of the most popular introductions to the New Testament are steeped in a Euro-Protestant-mythological interpretation that focuses not on pluralism but on a singular way of looking at history and of appropriating the documents. When I read it, it reminds me of my days at college when there was only "one" answer and one "interpretation."

Many popular textbooks reaffirm the traditional hegemony that has dominated biblical interpretation for most of the twentieth century. They reflect a monistic, hierarchical, ego-centered, and self-aggrandizing approach to studying the

Bible. There is an implicit appeal to superiority that some would term "biblical imperialism." It sidelines the revolutionary aspects of the Bible for a strategy that bolsters the author's own cultural standards, religious beliefs, and practices.

Many biblical scholars are caught in this historical-critical-mythological trap. And I think the basis for this trap finds its origins in the belief systems of the researchers. The locus of revelation for them is in the historical reconstruction of the situation of the texts. Finding the exact place and moment when Paul penned a letter to Corinth is the same quest that has been going on for a (it seems like) century by the people who want to discover the exact movements and words of Jesus. Our study and teaching of the documents must evolve out of the ideological into the cultural, creative, oral, socio-economic, and political realm. When scholars attempt to maintain the rigid practice of rehearsing historical reconstruction, this only serves to avoid the present real-time, and ignores the relevancy of the documents to a worldwide audience.

Inclusion and Internationalism

Feminist studies must embrace pluralism and internationalism as the most legitimate, fair, and honest way of studying the texts. Historical

criticism and the children it has produced is/are only one small facet of biblical studies. The old methods can no longer dominate the future of our discipline.

Consider the types of scholarship that are coming out of Asia and the Americas such as the Mujerista interpretation being developed by Latina biblical scholars. *The African Bible* challenges us to open our eyes to the "color" of the characters in the Bible. Alice Walker, Bell Hooks, and Delores Williams bid us to consider the Bible from a black woman's or Womanist perspective.

Post-colonial interpreters have begun dissecting traditional biblical scholarship and use words such as dehumanizing, pseudo-objectivity, color politics, Christian imperialism, legislative, exploitative, nationalistic, anti-Canaanite, anti-Jewish, combative, ideologically abusive, and fundamental, to describe popular-traditional-historical-critical scholarship. They want to decode what they term "imperialistic" texts of the bible that have silenced multiple voices. They have experienced a kind of "savagery" perpetrated by the reigning elitist interpreters and writers. And that savagery has been extended to gays and lesbians who have had the courage to boldly look at the texts through the eyes of a non-heterosexual. The door that they are knocking upon must be opened.

Compassion for Our Audience

Thirty years ago it was "liberating" to highlight the injustices perpetrated against females in the academy and the workplace. But times have changed, and feminists need to rethink their teaching strategies in the classroom. In my opinion, teaching feminist interpretation, and feminist interpretation of the documents only, is on very shaky ground in a state university. To impose a "Christian" feminist ideology on our students is close to the establishment of a "religion."

Students resent the feminist ideological position. The situation in the life of a professor and her students has changed. Even in the Midwest the ethnic landscape is becoming more diverse. Over 10% of my students were from other countries. Most students have been influenced by religions but they are not steeped in the traditions of the western Bible. Many have never read it.

Where do we begin the discussion about the documents? And how ethical is it for a "successful" female professor to discuss the awful effects of patriarchy, when male students and professors, gays and lesbians, remain unemployed and marginalized themselves? It remains a dilemma for me. And while I, even at this moment, feel the sting of the "patriarchy" in my own university, I am increasingly uncomfortable when I focus upon the singular issue of women. It seems to me that I am socializing my students into my own struggle, my own experience of abuse, and my own history of dealing with male supremacy.

Feminism must embrace -- not distance or dominate--the 'other.' A politic of inclusion, pluralism, and empowerment for all peoples must guide our interpretative strategies, if we are to make the case for relevancy of the biblical documents for all of our students.

Works Consulted

William L. Andrews, *Sisters of the Spirit: Three Black Women's Autobiographies of the Nineteenth Century* (Bloomington: Indiana University Press, 1986).

Mukti Barton, "The Skin of Miriam Became as White as Snow: The Bible, Western Feminism and Colour Politics," *Feminist Theology* 27(2001): 68-80.

Mark G. Brett, *Genesis: Procreation and the Politics of Identity* (London: Rutledge, 2000).

_____, *Ethnicity and the Bible* (Leiden: Brill Academic Publishers, 2002).

Musa W. Dube, ed., *Other Ways of Reading: African Women and the Bible* (Geneva: WCC Publications, 2001).

_____, *Postcolonial Feminist Interpretation of the Bible* (St. Louis: Missouri: Chalice Press, 2000).

Joan Chamberlain Engelsman, *The Feminine Dimension of the Divine* (Philadelphia: Westminster Press, 1979).

Elisabeth Schüssler Fiorenza, *Wisdom Ways: Introducing*

Feminist Biblical Interpretation (New York: Orbis Books, 2001).

Sean Freyne and Ellen van Wolde, eds., *The Many Voice of the Bible* (London: SCM Press, 2002).

M. Esther Harding, *Woman's Mysteries: Ancient and Modern* (New York: Harper, 1971).

Ursula King, ed., *Feminist Theology and the Third World, A Reader* (London: Orbis, 1994).

Jean K. Kim, "Uncovering Her Wickedness: An Inter (con)textual Reading of Revelation 17 from Postcolonial Feminist Perspective," *Journal for the Study of the New Testament* 73 (1999): 61-81

Gerda Lerner, *The Creation of Feminist Consciousness: From the Middle Ages to Eighteen-Seventy* (New York: Oxford University Press, 1993).

Kwok Pui-Lan and Elisabeth Schüssler Fiorenza, *Women's Sacred Scriptures* (London: SCM Press, 1998).

Ann Loades, ed., *Feminist Theology*: A Reader (London: SPCK, 1990).

Itumeleng J. Mosala, *Biblical Hermeneutics and Black Theology in South Africa* (Grand Rapids: William B. Eerdmans, 1989).

Heikki Raisanen, *Reading the Bible in the Global Village* (Helsinki, Atlanta: Society of Biblical Literature, 2000).

Luise Schottroff, Silvia Schroer, and Marie-Theresa Wacker, *Feminist Interpretation: The Bible In Women's Perspective* (trans. Martin and Barbara Rumscheidt; Minneapolis: Fortress, 1998).

Marla J. Selvidge, *Daughters of Jerusalem* (Scottsdale, Pennsylvania: Herald Press, 1987).

_____, *Notorious Voices: Feminist Biblical Interpretation, 1500-1920* (New York: Continuum, 1996).

_____. *Woman, Violence, and the Bible* (Lewiston: Edwin Mellen Press, 1996).

_____. *Luke the Feminist: A Study of Luke's Presentation of the Women in Luke-Acts* (M.A. thesis, *Wheaton College, 1973*).

25

_____. *The New Testament: A Timeless Book for All Peoples* (New Jersey: Prentice Hall, 1999).

_____. *Exploring the New Testament* (New Jersey, Prentice Hall, 2003).

_____. *Woman, Cult, and Miracle Recital: A Redactional-Critical Investigation of Mark 5:24-34* (London: Bucknell University Presses, 1990).

R. S. Sugirtharajah, *The Bible in the Third World. Pre-colonial, Colonial, and Postcolonial Encounters* (Cambridge: Cambridge University Press, 2001).

_____, ed., *Voices from the Margin: Interpreting the Bible in the Third World* (New York: Orbis, 1991).

Section Two
Misogynist Politics for a
Thousand Years

Chapter One
The Secrets of Women and *The Dead Sea Scrolls*
A Comparative and Theoretical Analysis

M isogyny and male supremacy incarnates itself in many forms, some of which may include, pornography, erotic literatures, and sexist laws. *Women's Secrets* (circa 1300 C.E.) contains disgusting underground blogs (text and comments) written by unknown males whose knowledge about female biological processes was taken from astrology, the Occult, magic, ancient philosophers, and petty observations. Their erotic observations may have functioned as pornography in their times. Helen R. Lemay argues that *Women's Secrets* (hereafter *Secrets)* laid the foundation for the *Malleus Maleficarum* which was used to imprison and kill females during the inquisition.[1] Written at least fifteen hundred years prior to *Secrets*, the *Dead Sea Scrolls* (circa 200 B.C.E.) exhibit some of the same misogynistic flavors. Within the purity laws and the poem, "*Wiles of the Harlot*," are words, laced with erotic intentions[2] that hope to isolate and malign women.

Chapter Two
Observations and Goals of this Analysis

This analysis will introduce you to *Secrets*, its contents, a theoretical author, and a summary of the three voices (Commentators A and B and Albert) on the topic of menstruation. Next, selected selections from the purity laws and *The Wiles of the Harlot* from the *Dead Sea Scrolls* are examined. Finally, this analysis summarizes comparisons and common points of contact regarding females among the literatures.

When studying *Secrets* to prepare for this analysis, echoes of the *Dead Sea Scrolls* kept coming into my mind. I had studied many of the Hebrew texts of the *Dead Sea Scrolls* while in graduate school and written papers evaluating the status of females, the *Scroll's* relationship to the *Gospel of John*, and differences found in the Masoretic (Hebrew) and Septuagint (Greek) texts. Those papers were never published. So I returned to the *Dead Sea Scrolls* and did indeed discover many similarities with *Secrets*.

Research began by analyzing every allusion or instance of menstruation discovered in the *Secrets*. After several readings (in English) I noticed that Commentators A and B within the *Secrets* differed with the original text ascribed to the author of the *Secrets*, Albert. Using a redactional-critical method, isolating texts describing menses in all three of the authors, different voices emerged.

After consulting several articles on the topic of "women and the *Dead Sea Scrolls (Scrolls)*" and finding little helpful information, I decided to focus on two different types of texts to analyze that of the "purity laws" and the poem, the *Wiles of the Harlot.*

I would argue the same conclusion reached by Blau and Sheres, "What we found was that among all of the books of the Bible copied by the sectarians at Qumran, the names, and often the deeds, of Biblical women were simply missing.... the blotting out of female names has interesting implications."[3]

Chapter Three
The Textual Tradition of *Secrets*

*S*ecrets was originally written in Latin with many manuscript editions. Attached to the *Secrets* are commentaries. In her excellent book, Women's *Secrets*, Dr. Lemay translates the texts into English while choosing selected commentaries (Commentary A and B) that circulated with the *Secrets*. The following analysis is based upon her translation and selected texts found in that book, *Women's Secrets. A Translation of Pseudo-Albertus Magnus" De Secretis Mulierum with Commentaries.* [4]

Literary Form: Cosmic Instructional Guide

Was the *Secrets* a manual for instruction or an underground treatise? Were they notes from an instructors class? Could they have been secret pornography for the celibate or homosexual? "If you keep this book to yourself, I promise to show you many things...."[5] The author of the *Secrets* writes in an authoritative scientific/philosophical tone about the female anatomy and its influence on males and culture, but more often than not, the conclusions and observations are pseudo-scientific or, what we would term, 'Science Fiction' today.[6]

There are many instances in the *Secrets* where the authors claim to have more knowledge than their readers. In Chapter III Albert (original text) takes up the topic of reasons for the origins of different types of human beings. The planets control the fetus in the womb and determine the race of the child. Blaming astrology and astronomy for his own racist views, he says, those planets "which the ancients call the gods of nature, [are] over the bodies and souls of men." [7]

Saturn will produce a person whom is "dark in color with flat, black hair, a tormented face ... malicious, irate, ... a wicked life. He likes foul smelling things, and is always dressed in dirty clothes." [8] Supposedly quoting Avicenna (a Persian scholar and medical doctor), they suggest that the hairs of a menstruating woman will produce a serpent if planted in the warm soil.[9] They look to the moon to control menses[10] and terrestrial matter as part and parcel of bone structure. Cosmic ideas permeate most pages of the texts as they describe how the planets control sex and reproduction.[1]

Chapter Four
Author: Adolescent Male
(Albert, himself)

Scholars have suggested, based upon internal evidence, that the original author of *Secrets* was a celibate cleric and wonder if the text was used in seminaries in Europe. To date no evidence has been discovered linking it with any institution of higher learning. Situating the blog(s) within a specific religious tradition is also problematic. While there are references to a "Christ," "To my dear companion and friend in Christ, may you be granted a long life filled with increasing wisdom," [12] perhaps one should avoid interpreting these sentences literally. Wisdom (Sophia) is also mentioned and this opening sentence could have been code language that alerted its readers that the texts were from the underground, or alternative universe signified by the word, "Wisdom," an ancient Jewish and Gnostic Goddess.

Commentary A author of the *Secrets* adds to the mystery by explaining or adding that Albert is writing for a priest who asked questions, and then later, identifies the author as a "Catholic." [13] The *Secrets* volume ends with an appeal, "Thus, I request that all my brothers who read this essay record their questions...." [14] But who are the "brothers?" Throughout the entire text there is very little evidence, if any, that people steeped in the traditions of Christianity, Judaism, or Islam authored these texts.

Whoever wrote *Secrets* does not appear to have intimate knowledge of (sex) or personal relationships with a females.[15] They have heard stories about menses and birth but none of them has a personal knowledge. [16] The writers were not medical doctors because they do not understand female anatomy. [17] They dabble in current and ancient mystical traditions and Islamic musings. The God that is described controls the planets and stars but does not intervene in the every day lives of people.[18]

After reading the *Secrets* many times, it seems logical to me to theorize that Albert is a hermaphrodite adolescent male who is going through puberty and prefers the company of males. The topic of hermaphrodites comes up in the discussion at least twice and Commentary A and B enlarges upon it. Albert muses about a child who is born with "two sets of sex organs, one male and one female, so that he could either lie underneath a sex partner or participate actively from the top." [19] That child could function as either sex but becoming a male is preferable. "The hermaphrodite is given the masculine species, for the male is worthier, although he really has both natures." [20]

Albert is from a wealthy family that provides tutors, and perhaps, some of those tutors are well acquainted with religions and philosophies outside the mainstream. *Secrets* answers many questions that might be asked by an adolescent male? How do you "do" sex?[21] How old should children be when they have sex?[22] Will it hurt when you have sex?[23] Will I lose my penis?[24] Can you contract a disease when you have sex?[25] Perhaps a friend had sex?[26] What about castrated males, eunuchs? What about sex with ejaculating animals?[27] What about lightning sex? [28] What about fat women, black women? [29] Will having lots of sexual encounters harm you? How do you know when a woman is menstruating? [30]

Albert obviously fears and detests females that are around him. Are they in control of him? Like a passive-aggressive child he hates being disciplined and has formed a morbid hatred for older females. "It should be noted that old women who still have their monthly flow, and some who do not menstruate, poison the eyes of children lying in their cradles by their glance." [31] And both Commentaries chime in with equally damaging comments about older females. Commentary A

34

contends that women can poison others but not themselves. [32] Commentary B continues, "Note that old women ought not to be permitted to play with children and kiss them, because they poison them to such a degree that sometimes they die." Commentary B exhibits a similar point of view, "[W]hy do menses kill children and not women themselves?[33] such words must come from people who fear older females. He wishes for their power over them to cease. Could *Secrets* have begun as random thoughts of a child who discussed dark and mysterious questions with friends having similar experiences and feelings.

Chapter Five
The Heart of *Secrets*

At the very center of the Albert's work there is an abhorrence of the female and everything associated with her. This abhorrence for the female anatomy and processes is not a new topic in ancient literatures. More than three decades ago, I researched Mark 5:24-34 and the significance of the Hemorrhaging Woman and concluded that "biology" was at the root of discrimination against females. [35]

To summarize *Secret's* view of menses is to

summarize the thoughts of a misguided and perhaps deranged person. The author and his commentators create a delusional world with regard to sexual relations and biological functions and dysfunctions. According to Lemay the purpose of *Secrets* is "to create in men a fear of the dangers of union with women."[36]

For Albert, menses is a food and can look like lead. Men should not have sex with women during their flux.[37] This advice may revert back to the concept of "niddah" (banishment) practiced by ancient and modern Jews, who separate themselves from menstruating females and vacated semen. (See the Dead Sea Discussion later.) Albert says, when females have sex with men, they use the males as a method to expel the menses fluid. [38] And "when men have sexual intercourse with these women it sometimes happens that they suffer a large wound and a serious infection of the penis because of iron that has been placed in the vagina...." [39]

The Voice of Commentary A

Unfortunately both of the Commentaries ratchet up the hype concerning menses when interpreting Albert's thoughts. Commentary A warns males that women in their menses poison animals, infect children, and give cancer and leprosy to males. [40] children who are conceived during sex with a woman in her menses "tend to have epilepsy and leprosy because menstrual matter is extremely venomous." [41] And beware, menses makes women crave sex.[42]

Sex with a menstruating woman is unclean and men should avoid it. [43] In a flurry of pages devoted to how males should not have sex with women because it shortens their life, he inserts a comment about how the menses of heavy women is black.[44] Supposedly quoting Hippocrates, he entreats males not to go near a menstruating woman because "the air is corrupted and the insides of man are brought to disorder." [45]

The Voice of Commentary B

Commentary B is more prolific on the topic of menses than the other two texts, creating myths that would warn males to stay away from females. Comparing anatomies, he asserts that the womb "is a masculine kind of organ" [46] and proceeds to compare semen with the fluid of menses. Women have female testicles. He takes up this topic later when discussing virginity. "There is a similarity in nature between the female breasts and the male testicles, for just as milk flows through the breasts, so the sperm is emitted through the testicals."[47] Quoting Aristotle, he states that "woman is a failed male ...woman is not human, but a monster in nature." [48]

Commentary B describes three types of menses. The first is the natural menses experienced by a female, next there is the supernatural experienced by Jews, and the third is "against nature" where Christians bleed through the anus and penis. [41]

Menses poisons any body it touches.[50] And he believes that women want to injure the penis with alum, lime or iron.[51] Some women want to eat testicles[52] and there are stories of females who slept with many kings and lords who were killed by females who had sex with them. Females are like poisonous animals, spiders, and snakes.[53]

Chapter Six
The *Dead Sea Scrolls*[54]

The Hebrew *Dead Sea Scrolls* found at Qumran in southern Israel, contain very little direct information about females who lived in the community. And while they predate the *Secrets* by at least 1500 years, they are written from a similar caustic point of view toward females. Identities of the writers and copiers of the documents are lost in the sands of the desert where they were purported to have been discovered by an Arab boy in 1946. Later documents dating to 1956 were discovered in nearby caves. Some contend the poem the *Wiles of the Harlot*, found at Qumran, should not be considered a product of the Dead Sea Community. Yet, it was discovered with other documents and so it belongs with them, no matter who created it.

Controversies have swirled around the identity of who occupied the community at Qumran and when it was occupied. Scholars argue over whether or not the community was all male and celibate or not. Did they have rituals that involved virgins? Were males castrated? [56] Remains of females have been discovered in the cemetery. Were they involved in community life? Was Qumran a sectarian or religious community that preserved these scrolls or were the scrolls hidden in the desert after the fall of the second temple. Since it appears that Qumran preserved ancient Israelite and Jewish documents, most scholars would attribute the works to a Jewish sect.

Chapter Seven
Purity Laws: *The Dead Sea Scrolls*

The following excerpts parallel *Secrets* in interpreting the natural biological processes in females as desecrating, as something that should not be touched. Defilement is at the center of these laws.

Purity Laws. 4Q274. Excerpt
Below is a paraphrase by Cynthia Bailey of *4Q274 Fragment 1 col.1*:

> 4 And she who is discharging blood, for seven days she may not touch the man who has a discharge or any of the objects that he uses. 5 Also for any of the objects he has laid on or sat on. And if she touches anything she will wash her clothes and bathe and afterwards she may eat. In no way may she mingle during her seven 6 days so she does not contaminate the camps of the holy ones of Israel. She may not touch any woman who has had a discharge of blood for several days. 7 And the one who is counting their seven days, whether they are male or female may not touch ... during the start of her period, unless she is clean from her menstruation. For the blood 8 from menstruation is considered a discharge for

anyone who touches it. And if a flow of semen is discharged, it is a misfortune. And he will be unclean... and anyone who touches 9 any of these unclean people, they will not eat during their seven days of their impurity, just like the person who is unclean through contact with a corpse. And they will bathe and wash and then... "[57]

These purity laws echo Leviticus 12-15. There is a fear of both blood and semen. Women who are menstruating must be kept in niddah or banishment for the full seven days. Touching unclean people is the same as touching a corpse. So, if the laws were enforced, females could not cook, take care of their children, work outside the home, or sleep with their husbands. They had to be cloistered.

Ita Sheres and Anne Kohn Blau, referring to the texts on purity, have studied Qumran and come to this conclusion about the Scrolls, "It is therefore plain that if there was a role for women to play at Qumran, it was secondary, subservient, and oppressive. [58] The most extensive discussion of women in the Qumran writings is in the Temple Scroll, where the author's main concern is with women's bodies, sexual purity, and cleanness, including their blood and nakedness. Menstruating women and those who just completed their confinement are not allowed to enter the battle camps.... [59]

Secrets, while not written as a legal document as 4Q274 repeatedly underscores the liabilities of the blood of menses or having sex with a woman who is menstruating. Secrets does not quote or refer to purity laws but appears to be interpreting similar prescriptions so that the reader understands all the ramifications of touching the 'unclean.' Qumran declares females to be unclean but Secrets take this one step further by claiming that menstruating women kill, cause harm to the penis, illness, and leprosy. "The womb of a female is like a sewer situated in the middle of a town where all the waste materials run together and are sent forth."[60]

Chapter Eight
The Wiles of the Harlot

The *Wiles of the Harlot* is a very provocative/erotic poem that leads the reader to imagine a sexual encounter on a long road to Jericho. Due to copyright limitations we cannot quote the entire poem, so we have chosen a small excerpt. The poem begins with describing the physical characteristics of a female from her lips to her feet. She is maligned, yet, is portrayed in terms that would attract readers to her. While the central theme of the "*Wiles*" is not menstruation, it describes the "gates" of a female and anyone who associates with those gates as going to hell, resonating with *Secrets* about the dangers of having sex with females.

The *Wiles of the Harlot*. 4Q184. An excerpt.

> 6 Her lodgings are couches of darkness and in the heart of the night are her tents. In the foundations of gloom she sets up her dwelling 7 and camps in the tents of silence. In the midst of eternal fire is her inheritance and those who shine do not enter. 8 She is the start of all the ways of wickedness. Alas! She is the ruination of all who inherit her, and the calamity of all those who grasp her. 9 For her paths are paths of death, and her roads, tracks to sin. Her trails lead astray toward wickedness, 10 and her pathways, to the guilt of transgression. Her gates are the gates of death, and in the entrance to her house, Sheol proceeds. 11 All those who go to her will not come back, and all those who inherit her will sink to the pit. 27 To sidetrack man into the paths of the pit, and seduce the sons of men with smooth words. [61]

Melissa Aubin, employing the tool of twenty-first century rhetoric analyzes this poem with severity. The heroine of the poem is "aggressive, foreign, deceitful and irreverent." [62] And so the female character becomes the "anti-type to Wisdom," i.e. the "Perfect Wife." "As the language of the poem fashions a thoroughly negative characterization of apostasy as Seductress, the rhetoric that props this language consistently repels the reader from her." [63]

The reader would only be repelled if he feared "hell" or believed the words were coming directly from a divine voice. I would argue, that although the language degrades and humiliates a female, it attracts the fantasy of a lonely male and propels him toward her, producing the opposite effect. *Wiles* lures the reader into fantastic space where he begins to 'want' what he cannot and should not have according to the author. It is a pathway to awakening 'lust.' [64] And lust is also at the center of *Secrets*.

Chapter Nine
Common Points of Contact
Secrets and the *Dead Sea Scrolls*

There are many points of contact between the *Wiles* and *Secrets*. The authors of both appear to be males. Both documents seem to have been written to instruct other students or males. Both are steeped in religions, while the *Wiles* appears to come out of a Jewish sect, *Secrets* dabbles in all sorts of cosmology with a touch of Christianity. Males are viewed as the 'normal' but females are 'othered' or deviant.

Itemized body Parts

Both literatures enjoy focusing upon female body parts and their dysfunction for males. While damning females the language itself is eroticized.

The Wiles
> [Her eyes} have been defiled with evil, her hands go down to the pit, her feet sink to act wickedly and to walk towards crimes. [65]

Secrets (Corruption of Virginity)
> Sometimes virgins are gravely corrupted so t hat their vagina is greatly enlarged because the male member is exceedingly large and

inept. When this happens the woman's vagina become so widened that the man can enter there without any pain to his member, and this is a sign that the woman was first corrupted.

It happened another time that a thunderbolt burned the pubic hairs, because a thunderbolt can penetrate the interior parts in the manner I have just described. [67]

Desecrating Touch

In page after page in *Secrets,* the authors argue for keeping a distance from females. And if you do have sex, don't have too much because children might be deformed or you might get a headache. Too much sex can kill you! [68]

The Wiles

Alas, she is the ruination of all who inherit her, and the calamity of all those who grasp her, " [69]

Secrets

It is harmful for men to have sexual intercourse with menstruating women because should conception take place the fetus would be leprous. This also frequently causes cancer in the male member." [7]

46

Sexual Prowess and Lack of Self-Control

Males don't really want to have sex; it is the females who trick them into doing it. Displaced anger explodes in this poem and the pages of *Secrets*. Melissa Aubin captures the moment,
"As sexual agent, she renders her lovers passive. But as a result of emasculating her victims, she is condemned by the narrator, as was Jezebel, who upset the dominance of the male gaze and haughtily looked upon her pursuers from a window before meeting a grisly fate." [71]

The Wiles

In the city squares she veils herself, and there is no one who interrupts her [her] incessant (fornicating). [72] For her paths are paths of death, and her roads, tracks to sin. Her trails lead astray towards   wickedness and   her   pathways,   to   the   guilt   of transgression. [73]

Secrets

External impediment is often found in harlots, who continuously receive a great deal of seed from men, so that the sperm of one man corrupts the womb when it meets the seed of another man."[74]

Resistance to Domesticity: The Gaze

All authors agree that a woman's glances can have lethal consequences upon a man's life. Her role in life is service to males. If she steps out of that role, she is castigated and feared.

The Wiles
> Her eyes scan hither and yon, and she raises her eyebrows impudently, to spot the just man and overtake him, and the important man, to trip him up.[75]

Secrets
> The signs of chastity are as follows: shame, modesty, fear, a faultless gait and speech, casting eyes down before men and the acts of men." [76]

Theoretical Summary and Conclusion

It seems like Science Fiction to imagine that people could live during times when literatures like the *Wiles*, the *Purity Laws*, and *Secrets* were produced. But, people live in and work in similar communities today where these types of literatures would be welcomed, where females are despised for their strength and controlled by the environment so that males are elevated, not threatened or harmed in any way. Misogyny, pornography, erotic literature, and sexist laws permeate cultures all over the globe.

Studying these documents may illicit profound anger and disgust in females. Conclusions can be drawn that suggest that documents like these served the greater purpose of imprisoning women by socializing them into a subservient existence. And, as Helen Lemay argues, lay a foundation for greater discrimination, harassment, and death. But they could also be read in another way.

Women had to find room to breathe, to function in a male dominated and centered society. These documents give some evidence that females did possess power over some males. Every time we uncover a law limiting females or books such as the *Secrets* that attempt to malign and defame females, we know that some females had power in society. (And just because we discover laws does not mean they were enforced. But what we do know is that males (presumably) wanted that control.) Some men feared women (for a variety of reasons) so they attempted to portray females in disgusting ways in order to control them. In spite of the misogyny and hopeful male supremacy we have discovered, we have also discovered (theoretically, indirectly) that some women may have used the very phobias that men had toward women to mitigate their power, and perhaps, exercise control over the males. One could only hope!

Notes
1 Helen Rodnite Lemay, *Women's Secrets. A Translation of Pseudo-Albertus Magnus's De Secretis Mulierum with Commentaries*, New York, 1992.
2 Florentino Garc'ia Martin'inez, *The Dead Sea Scrolls Translated. The Qumran Texts in English*, Leiden, 1994, Second Edition.
3 Anne K. Blau and Ita Sheres, *Women Anonymous: The Dead Sea Scroll's Gender Legacy* in *Centennial Review* 39(1995), p.147.
4 The name of Albert will denote the main text with Commentary A and B referred to independently.
5 Lemay, p. 59
6 Science Fiction, according to the online Miriam Webster Dictionary, 'is fiction dealing principally with the impact of actual or imagined science on society or individuals or having a scientific factor as an essential orienting component.' http://www.merriamwebster.com/dictionary/science+fiction?show=0&t=1295276209
7 Lemay, p. 91
8 Lemay, p. 91
9 Lemay, p. 96 and Laleh Bakhtiar, *The Canon of Medicine*, Chicago, 1999.
10 Lemay, p. 89
11 Lemay, p. 80-81
12 Lemay p. 12
13 Lemay p. 84
14 Lemay, p. 148
15 Lemay, p. 17
16 Lemay, p. 17

17 Lemay, p. 5
18 Lemay, p. 30
19 Lemay, p. 19
20 Lemay, pp. 20, 116
21 Lemay, pp. 73, 102, 114
22 Lemay, p. 77
23 Lemay, p. 88
24 Lemay, p. 121
25 Lemay, p. 88
26 Lemay, p. 26
27 Lemay, p. 116
28 Lemay, p. 105
29 Lemay, p. 136
30 Lemay, p. 130
31 Lemay, p. 120
32 Lemay, pp. 120, 130
33 Lemay, p. 131
34 Andrew Shail and Gillian Howie, *Menstruation. A Cultural History*, New York, 2005. No specific pages.
35 Marla J. Selvidge, *Woman, Cult, and Miracle Recital. A Redactional-Critical Investigation* of Mark 5:24-34, New Jersey, 1990 (Dissertation, 1980).
36 Lemay, p. 16
37 Lemay, p. 128
38 Lemay, p. 132
39 Lemay, p. 88
40 Lemay, 40
41 Lemay, 129
42 Lemay, 121
43 Lemay, 60
44 Lemay, 44
45 Lemay, 89 In this analysis I use the word "supposedly" because I tried without success to track down quotations from Avicenna and Averroes. Lemay, pp. 43ff had the same problem with Albert's allusion to

Scholars.
46 Lemay, p. 70
47 Lemay, p. 73
48 Lemay, p. 106
49 Lemay, p. 71
50 Lemay, 75
51 Lemay, 89
52 Lemay, 122
53 Lemay, 131
54 Marti'nez. See FN #2.
55 4Q184, Marti'nez, pp. 379-380
56 Ita Sheres and Anne Kohn Blau, *The Truth About the Virgin*, New York, 1995.
57 Story of the *Dead Sea Scrolls*:
        http://religiousstudies.uncc.edu/people/jtabor/DSSEs say.htm Cynthia Bailey: Ritual Purity Laws (4QTohorot-a)

        http://ccat.sas.upenn.edu/humm/Resources/StudTxts /4Q274.html (2 of 3)2006-08-01 12:14:56
        http://www.documentacatholicaomnia.eu/o3d/sineda ta,_Absens,_Dead_Sea_Scroll_%5BTexts_An d_Translations%5D,_EN.pdf
58 Sheres, p. 40
59 Sheres, p. 39
60 Lemay, pp. 133-134
61 Marti'nez, p. 61
62 Melissa Aubin, *"She is the Beginning of all Ways of Perversity:' Femininity and Metaphor in 4Q184"* in *Women in Judaism: A Multidisciplinary Journal* 2(2001), p. 2. See another article, Eileen M. Schuller, *"Women in the Dead Sea Scrolls"* in *Annals of the New York Academy of Sciences* (2006), pp. 116-131.
63 Aubin, p.11
64 Aubin, p. 11. "In a characteristically feminine way, she is

out of control, but at the same time she is tacitly masculinized by emitting the spiked protusions of sharp words, an image elsewhere found in descriptions of evil men (Psalms 64:4; 104:4; 1QH 5:13) whose sword-like words are martial." Aubin notes that "feet" within the poem are a euphemism for the penis (Isaiah 7:20; Ruth 3:7; Exodus 4:25). Scholars often interpret ancient texts that refer to "she" or a "female" literally. It crossed my mind while studying this poem that the "she" may have used metaphorically for a "he," a male prostitute. Descriptions of the female anatomy are masculinized in such a way that may have been interpreted by the reader or hearer as a male. Could we interpret this poem through the eyes of a transexual also?

65 Marti'nez, p. 379
66 Lemay, p. 126
67 Lemay, p. 104
68 Lemay, p. 127
69 Lemay, p. 69
70 Lemay, p. 131
71 Aubin, p. 19
72 Marti'nez, p. 380
73 Marti'nez, p. 379
74 Lemay, 137
75 Marti'nez, p. 380
76 Lemay, p. 128

Section Three
The Politics of Interpretations
Chapter One
Which Biblical Documents? Which Translation?

The choice of texts or translations of the Bible can predict the interpretative outcome for researchers. Before we begin our discussion on feminist biblical interpretation we must acknowledge that not every Bible contains the same contents nor is translated using the same vocabulary or belief system. The reader may not be aware of some of the following documents. My apologies, but every reader of the Bible should be aware of these important literary pieces.

No translation is "objective." The *Septuagint*, a two thousand year old Greek "translation" of Hebrew documents, differs with the *Masoretic Text* (Hebrew text) in number, order, and scope of the documents listed. (Although some scholars argue that the *Septuagint* should stand-alone and is not a translation.) Should the Jewish and Christian Apocrypha be designated as biblical documents? Reformers such as Martin Luther rejected biblical writings that included the Book of Revelation and James, while modern translations, for example, from the Jehovah's Witnesses; omit certain texts that are found in what scholars have determined to be the best Greek manuscripts that form the accepted basis of the New Testament.

What about literatures such as the *Dead Sea Scrolls* and the *Nag Hammadi* collection? [1] The *Dead Sea Scrolls* contain copies of biblical texts found in the Masoretic collection (Old Testament) or documents related to the growth of religious communities. What about the Samaritan manuscripts housed at Michigan State University?

Should the Talmud, Mishnah, and Gemara be on our list? And is the Islamic Qur'an's appropriation of biblical stories fair game? Now which translation should we use when we study these documents? And what about the selection of the Greek documents that was finally included in the "canon?" Who collected them and why did they collect them and did they have a bias towards or against certain traditions?

Chapter Two
No Single Point of View in the Bible

The biblical documents present varying and contrasting views on many topics. Paul, a writer of several documents in the New Testament, seems to have a different view of those who witnessed Jesus after the resurrection in I Corinthians 12 than the stories found in the gospels. And the gospels themselves differ as to the timing and people involved in the death and resurrection of Jesus. The synoptics (Gospels of Matthew, Mark, and Luke) rehearse many similar stories but their points of view and outcomes differ. Even their language changes the stories. There are open and inviting views of Christianity in some of Paul's letters. "There is no Jew, no Gentile, no slave, no free, no male, no female..." (Galatians 3:28) but there are also narrow views in identifying the "real" Christian in the pseudo-Pauline letters. Acts of the Apostles paints a fantastic story about an explosion of converts in early Christianity while at the same time disparaging Jews and chronicling the abuse that Paul gave and experienced. So it should not surprise anyone that there are many different types of interpretations of the biblical documents because the Bible houses many voices.

Chapter Three
Defining Feminist Biblical Interpretation

The term "feminist biblical interpretation" is almost anachronistic in the twenty-first century. While the term "feminist biblical interpretation" is a literary construct of the twentieth century, its aims and goals were embraced by many throughout history. In the twenty-first century the fields and methodologies of feminist inquiry have mushroomed at such a capacity that defining the above term is almost impossible. Now there are hundreds of sub-fields that claim primacy.

For example, does "feminist biblical interpretation" mean that the researcher will limit herself to only females and female issues? Is it a singular point of view or a single methodological approach to the documents? What does it mean to be a feminist? What is the purpose or purposes of this type of interpretative approach?   Can we outline the approach? And are we interpreting the Bible with the attempt to reconstruct the historical past or create meaning for the present? Below are selected trajectories of attempts to define the term.

In 1979 Elizabeth Fox-Genovese characterized feminist criticism as, "Confronting a male-dominated culture, feminist critics must at once elucidate that domination, disengage the strategies available to women within their imprisoning otherness, and assess the possibilities for translating, transforming, and appropriating the dominate cultural tradition as a heritage for women as well as men."[2] Yet she also argues that "there are many feminisms, so there are many feminist interpretations." [3]   She condemns feminist orthodoxy. "Feminist interpretation charts the relationship of the bond to their bondage. In so doing, it deconstructs-translates, transforms, and appropriates   --the   dominant   subjective consciousness of man."[4]

Pamela J. Milne, in "No promised Land: Rejecting the Authority of the Bible," argues, "one of our principal feminist goals must be to ensure that the biblical text does not have the devastating effects on women's lives in the future that it has had in the past."[5] T. Drorah Setel comments, "On a historical level, feminist biblical scholarship affirms the significance of female experience throughout human history."[6]

Elisabeth Schüssler Fiorenza describes feminist biblical interpretation as "a ... struggle over authority, values, and meaning."[7] In *Wisdom Ways*, she writes, "I am concerned here with engaging in a social critique and political analysis of biblical traditions and contemporary discourses that is verified pragmatically through its contribution to an increase in liberation and well-being."[8] Most recently an entry in the *Handbook of Biblical Interpretation* defines feminist biblical criticism as a criticism that "seeks to give voice to what has been silenced or ignored and what is necessary for any complete understanding of God, scripture, and humankind."[9]

Some interpreters define the goals of feminist biblical interpretation as transforming the current social structures or rescuing those who are victimized by society. They want to disprove or undermine the "male" perspective concerning females. Many place the blame for violence against females and children on the myth of a God who allowed his own son to die. "The image of God the Father demanding and carrying out the suffering and death of his own son has sustained a culture of

59

abuse and led to the abandonment of victims of abuse and oppression." [10] The goals and strategies are limitless.

Chapter Four
Feminist Methodologies and Commentary

Most short histories of feminist biblical interpretation begin with the 1848 Seneca Falls Convention. This gathering of women was a landmark attempt at raising the issues of equity in the Americas, but it was not the beginnings of feminist biblical interpretation. And Leonard Swidler's "Jesus was a Feminist," was an early catalyst in the twentieth century for others to begin to look at individual writers of the Bible and their points of view. [11]

It is difficult to create an accurate history or summary of feminist biblical interpretation because so many historic feminist voices are being discovered and included in the body of literature that we have today. While we could attempt to demonstrate the sequenced historical development of the methodologies, this time line would also be inaccurate because so many developing methodologies overlapped or were reconstructed using primary material from the historically earlier interpreters.

Surveying the vast array of approaches under the umbrella of feminist biblical interpretation can be instructive. Researchers may use traditional exegetical or interpretative methodologies or create one of their own. Some scholars attempt to reduce feminist biblical interpretation to a few key terms, categories, or grids.[12] Those tables or grids are reductionistic and minimize the diversity within feminist biblical interpretative approaches, so I have constructed general categories without rigid rules. Below are columns with alphabetical list of some of the feminist biblical interpretative strategies that may overlap, be combined together, or stand-alone. The list is not exhaustive. See the next page.

61

Traditional Methods[13]
Archaeology
Canonical Criticism
Cultural Criticism
Form Criticism
Historical Criticism
Language Analysis
Literary Criticism
Midrash
Narrative Criticism
Reader Response
Criticism
Redaction Criticism
Source Criticism
Structural Exegesis
Textual Criticism
Translation as
Interpretation

Newer Methods/Strategies
African Reading of the
Bible
Asian Feminist
Interpretation
Cultural Relativistic
Approach
De-Patriarchalizing
Dialectical Feminist
Discovering Female
Voices
Divination Method
Ethnological and
Anthropological
Evolutionary Criticism

Female as the Ideal Sex
Female Centered
Interpretation
Female Characters in the
Text
Female Images of the
Divine
Feminist Criticism
Feminist Proof-Texting
Feminist Social Criticism
Gendering a Text
Gender Criticism
Gender Stereotyping
Global Feminist Biblical
Studies
Hermeneutic of Culture
Idealized
Ideological Criticism
Inclusive Methodologies
Invisible Women in the
Text
Japanese Feminist
Interpretation
Korean Feminist
Interpretation
Latina Feminist
Interpretation
Loyalist
Male Bias
Marxist-Feminist
Criticism
Material Feminism
Mestizo/a Consciousness
New Black Feminist
Criticism
New Testament Use of

Hebrew Bible Female
Characters
Pakistani Feminist
Interpretation of the Bible
Post Colonial
Interpretation
Post-Modern Biblical
Criticism
Post Structural Feminism
Psychoanalytical Feminist
Criticism
Reader-Oriented
Interpretations
Reader Response
Criticism
Recreating Female History
Recovering Female
History
Rejectionist
Revisionist
Signifying Scriptures
Slave Narrative
Interpretation
Socialist
Social Scientific Criticism
Structures of Dominance
Status of Females in the
Text
Transgendered Criticism
Transnational Feminist
Critique
Womanist or Women of
Color
Women as Authors of the
Text

Social/Political Commentary

Art and Criticism of
Patriarchy
Biblical Foundations of
Violence
Biblical Foundations of
Violence against
Females/Children
Bibliodrama
Culture of Impotence
Disability Interpretation
Divine Females
Eco-Feminism
Exploitation
Female as Christ
Female
Enslavement/Confinemet
Females as Priests
Feminist Theology of
Liberation
Human Rights Activism
Idolatry of the male
Inclusive Bible
Jewish Law (Halakhah)
and Women
Liberation Theology
Marginalization of
Feminist Ideas
Misogynistic Interpreters
and Interpretations
Patriarchal and
Colonizing Translations
Projecting values into the
Past

Queer Theory
Roots of Anti-feminism
Sexual Politics
Sexist Language
Same-sex Marriage
Story Theology
Structures of Dominance
Women as Leaders

Chapter Five
The Politics of Feminism and Male Supremacy

"Whoever fights monsters should see to it that in the process he does
not become a monster."[xiv]   F. W. Nietzsche

When studying apocalyptic biblical literatures we learn that there are hierocrats (those in power) and visionaries (those who want power).[xv] For as long as there have been biblical documents the struggle for power has ensued. When people link arms with a single solitary God discovered in the Bible, they can assume powerful positions (social, psychological, political, economic) over others. Recent feminist scholarship has developed many tools to attempt to wrench away the power that some have had over the biblical texts and those who study them.

For millennia, females heard about and studied the Bible in ways that often socialized them into a belief and social system of male supremacy. The Bible was interpreted primarily by males for males. And that male belief system influenced and controlled social behavior, psychological view of self, career and political opportunities of women in society. (It is also encased and punished women by placing them in social, psychological, economic, and literal prisons for being different.) Some females accepted the belief in male supremacy/male interpretation while others began to ask their own questions of the text because the realities expounded by those in power did not synchronize with female experience or spiritual needs.

To assume that the interpretative structure that was primarily initiated by males was not legitimated by consenting females is an erroneous conclusion. For an interpretative method or interpretation to be normative most people within the community must accept it. The beliefs stemming from an accepted interpretation can become symbols that function to solidify and form a basis for an identity within a community. Some females supported and accepted the patriarchal interpretative systems and even employed them in their written and artistic works.[xvi] Many females approved of and linked to this power of male interpretation gaining status, power, and recognition from it. They enjoyed their status because it gave them a defined role that they believed originated within the Divine Voice housed in the biblical documents.

Feminist discoveries during the *mid-twentieth* century that males interpreted a male-conceived and male created Bible were startling for some. Male was viewed as normative or supreme, society was patriarchal, therefore females were invisible and oppressed. Some believed the Bible to be more inclusive, and so, set about translating and interpreting the Bible to prove it was pluralistic. Others focused on discovering important stories about invisible or unnamed females in the Bible, or individual author's points of view regarding females, and engaged in the speculation that some of the Biblical texts were written by females.

The 1979 feminist classic *Womanspirit Rising. A Feminist Reader in Religion* edited by Carol Christ contains diverse articles stemming from Christianity, Judaism, Paganism, and the worship of Goddesses. The collection questions a male view of "sin," psychological theory, history, and the foundational belief in a triumphant God. It implies that God needs a sex change. The writers explore experimental ways of interpreting the Bible by focusing upon females and writing for females. They dared to ask the Goddess question, and pointed readers to religions outside the mainstream to Starhawk and Paganism as more welcoming and productive for females.[xvii]

During this historic time period hundreds of books were produced featuring many different types of investigations. The 1985 collection of interpretations by Letty Russell suggested that "scriptures need liberation, not only from existing interpretations but also the patriarchal bias of the text themselves." [xviii]   Both male and female interpreters, in the twentieth century, began to successfully erode the traditional foundation of patriarchal interpretations of biblical texts. And while many denominations had ordained women since the mid-nineteen century, (1853 Antoinette Brown, a Congregational minister); pressure was placed upon Roman Catholicism, divisions within Judaism, and other denominations to ordain females. Both the Reform and Conservative Jewish congregations began to ordain female Rabbis toward the second half of the twentieth century.

Feminist scholarship in the *late twentieth century* began to ask questions of the text that produced a plethora of methodologies and questions. They uncovered male bias and control of interpretation of the texts within and external to the texts themselves. They also found misogyny, brainwashing, exploitation, female objectification, scapegoatism, violence, dehumanization, marginalism, male supremacy, imperialism, and hegemony.

Chapter Six
Misandry and Feminism

In the process of discovering and attacking male dominance, some of the early feminist interpreters of the twentieth century made the same mistakes as their male peers. They aimed at controlling interpretation and therefore assuming power over the documents and social agenda. Some appeared to be dogmatic with interpretations taking on a "fundamental" flare, "our way is the only way." Their point of view was narrowly focused on feminist interpretations featuring females and female concerns.

Feminist works were also sometimes anti-Semitic, lacking sensitivity to people of color or other ethnic groups, under-developed countries, classes, and sexual orientations. Alice Walker, bell hooks, and Rita J. Weems, and many others helped to unearth this "hidden" prejudice and white supremacy.

For the remainder of the latter part of the twentieth and into the twenty-first century feminist scholars focused their interpretative strategies upon the goal of eroding the power of the "patriarchy," termed "kyriarchy" by Elisabeth Schüssler Fiorenza.

The pejorative term "malestream" (an obvious play on words featuring the male anatomy) seems to permeate recent literature of the twenty-first century. More often than not, "patriarchy," a word that stems from Greek meaning "rule of the father, or father-ruler" equated to males, all males. And this study of patriarchy has often led to the hatred of males or misandry, says Patrick M. Arnold. Arnold took on the feminists, while agreeing with their premises; he told them that they had taken their arguments too far by targeting and discriminating against males. Females had taken positions at key institutions and had mimicked the same type of behavior as the males. The only difference now was that it was "matriarchal."[xix]

Chapter Seven
Biblical Interpretation on Every Corner

Women have always, since the invention of the biblical documents, attempted to discover meaning within its pages. Elizabeth Cady Stanton lamented that female scholars with training in biblical languages would not participate in the "Women's Bible" project.[xx] Today we understand that Stanton did not need those specialists in languages to write a commentary, because the languages often offer little help in understanding the relevancy and application of a passage for and about females in modern times.

Twenty-first century researchers are analyzing varieties of literatures that interpreted the Bible from a feminist perspective that many excluded in the early stages of research. Their review includes analyzing letters, poems, hymns, children's literature, novels, plays, art, stained glass windows, archaeological data, images of Mary; how the New Testament writers use the stories of female characters found in the Hebrew Bible; and more, in order to discover how the authors employed and interpreted the Bible in the past and present.

Chapter Eight
Feminist Biblical Interpretation through Time
Were they Proto-Feminists?

Phyllis Trible's "Depatriarchalizing in Biblical Interpretation,"[xxi] sent shock waves through the academy when she characterized Adam in the story of the garden in Genesis as "passive, brutish, and inept," while at the same time lauding Eve as "intelligent, sensitive, and ingenious." She was using traditional methods to challenge one of the most damning and theologically important passages of scripture used by biblical scholars to "blame" Eve for all the "evil" in the world. Her conclusions seemed new yet throughout history we know that some people have always recognized the importance of power over females over others and set about speaking their minds about it. Trible's ideas had been proffered in the past, but perhaps it was the optimum time to publish them again. If we study history we know that people have argued against patriarchal interpretation and domination since the invention of the Bible. Among the first of these people were the "ammas."

During the formative years of Christianity, it was the desert mothers who challenged the locals to pay attention to females. Early hermits (males) and ammas (females) spent much of their lives shut up in caves or in rooms in convents as a way of drawing attention to injustices and problems that they viewed within Christianity. While there is no evidence that these fine people studied the ancient languages of the biblical texts, they did interpret them by the way they lived and the advice they gave to others. (Some classify this methodology today as "signifying.")

Similar to the females who became nuns/sisters within convents these hearty women preferred an alternate existence to the accepted "patriarchal" society that limited their choice of careers and education. Some had great fortunes that they shared with others before they took up the practice of praying. They drew attention to the fact that females could also be a voice from the Divine. They who had sacrificed everything proved that females could lead very different kinds of lives. They redefined the female role that was expected of them by their family and religious environment.

Sarah of the Desert said, "I am a woman but not according to my thoughts," to two old men who wanted to humiliate her.[xxii] Of course, we have no evidence that any of these statements came directly from the person to whom they are attributed. But they are indicative of a point of view during that time period. She knew too well how females were treated and so challenged them to think outside their narrow minds. She also said, "It is I who am a man, you who are women," to a group of monks.[xxiii] Both of her statements upset the standard way of measuring the worth of a person while highlighting that females could achieve and become more than males.

Many historic groups and people recognized some of the same sexist and patriarchal problems that modern scholarship has investigated. The Beguines, Cistercians, Cathars and Waldensians interpreted the Bible in such a way as to allow females to attain to the highest level within their organizations. Mystics, such as Julian of Norwich, during the middle Ages saw images of God as Mother, and so, followed her kinder and gentler path.

Alcun Blamires, in *Woman Defamed and Woman Defended. An Anthology of Medieval Texts*, captures texts from the tenth to the fifteen-century that he entitles, "Responses to Antifeminism." Included in that list are *Abelard, Albertano of Brescia, John Gower, The Trial of Walter Brut*, and more. Says Abelard, "Weigh carefully the dignity of woman, by whom Christ was twice anointed during His life, both on the feet and on the head.... It was the women, spending a sleepless night at his sepulcher that deserved to be first to see the glory of the risen Christ. More in their actions than in their words, they showed Him, by their loyalty at His death, how much they had loved Him during His life...." [xxiv] You have only to enter the doors of cathedrals in Italy (Florence and Venice), Belgium, the Netherlands, and Spain, to recognize the power of the image of a female over a sometimes corrupt church bureaucracy. Also study the art and images of the female who overarches the small figures of Jesus in those same cathedrals. [xxv]

This quest for equality with a hint toward superiority reaches all the way back to people such as; the Grimké Sisters, George and Margaret Fell

Fox (Quakers), Lucretia Mott, Phoebe Palmer, Barbara Kellison, Mary Hays, Antionette Blackwell, Heinrich Agrippa, Mary Astell, Frances Willard, and Julia Evelina Smith who translated both the Hebrew Bible and New Testament into English. Early in the nineteenth century, Maria W. Miller Steward, a free black, wrote about a "white" nation that had "caused the daughters of Africa to commit whoredoms and fornications; but upon thee be their curse." She called for a veiled war against her oppressors.[xxvi]

Many historic interpreters taught equality even superiority of the female. None of these people achieved Ph.D.'s in Biblical Languages or Literature or Theology, but all the same, they interpreted the Bible in a feminist and often-revolutionary way. For instance, Anna Bonus Kingsford and Edward Maitland wrote of a male and female god that provided insight for a branch of Theosophy in England during the nineteenth century. Later, Christian Science founder, Mary Baker Eddy also viewed the Divine as female. The Unity School of Christianity taught that the Divine was both male and female under the direction of Charles and Myrtle Fillmore. Mother Ann Lee, leader within the Shaker movement during the 18th century, viewed herself as the incarnation or female image of the Jesus.

Joanna Southcott, in the 18th century, preached that she was the savior, the woman clothed with the sun. She was to liberate them from the awful males who controlled the lives of her constituents. Her followers were mesmerized, "Our eyes were so dazzled with the glorious prospect set before us ... we became like the man taken out of the dark room ... the light so overpowering him that he could not see ... the idea of having of the GODHEAD to reign over us was overwhelming, after so long tyrannized over by man...."[xxvii]

Charlotte Perkins Gilman, during 19th century, surely was critiquing the patriarchal Bible when she penned *Herland*, a novel that situated "birthing" not "sacrifice" at the center of her imagined female-run world. [xxviii] Only females inhabit a world that is peaceful and utopian. Females give birth to only females without males. They are strong, intelligent, and run their own society, something that is not articulated in either of the Testaments.

Matilda Joslyn Gage's nineteenth century work, *Woman, Church and State*, reads as if it could have been written today. She argued that Christianity and specifically males, the patriarchate in Christianity, claimed divine right to control and exploit females.[xxix] Her work and unique writing style reverberates in, Mary Daly's, *The Church and the Second Sex* who also studied the feminist French philosopher Simone de Beauvoir's, *The Second Sex*.[xxx]

Freed slaves also interpreted the Bible. Sojourner Truth has been quoted often with her story about stripping open her blouse and exclaiming, "Ain't I a woman!" while she recounted her struggle and strength as a slave equal to any male. But there are other voices from slaves that are being discovered these days. Emerson B. Powery, in his article, "'Rise Up, Ye Women': Harriet Jacobs and the Bible," reveals that slaves did experience sexual abuse and were often caught in the middle between master and wife with patriarchy winning the conflict. Powery concludes, "Jacobs offers us a sensitivity to interpretation that places her among the predecessors of feminist engagement with the Bible as much as a forerunner of black hermeneutics. She is, indeed, an early proto-womanist interpreter of the Bible."[xxxi]

Many other works by feminist scholars are emerging. For instance, Katharine Bushnell's extraordinary life and work was lost in obscurity for decades, relegated to oblivion. She was original, talented, and analytically astute. In a list of one hundred topics in the 1921 *God's Word to Women*, she attacks male bias in the Bible by featuring their historical prejudice and methodologies that she claims are inaccurate. Her term for this was "Sex Bias." She views males as selfish, uncaring, and arrogant. In most of her translations and interpretations she uses a historical-critical method to disprove misconceptions. For example she argues that the women served at the tabernacle for the Israelites. They were priestesses or Levites. Quoting scholars of her time, she says they mistranslated and misinterpreted the role of the priestesses as "serving women" when they were actually leaders within the ancient Israel.[xxxii]

Lee Anna Starr, in 1926, wrote about male prejudice and their distortion of Scriptures regarding females. Assuming that the Bible is historical and that dispensational categories are correct, she interprets passages relevant to women by examining different translations and interpreters. Her God was not a sexist. She concludes, "He set at naught every man-imposed restriction on woman. He recognized no double standard: with Him there was no such thing as a preferred sex."[xxxiii]

Chapter Nine
Newer Methodologies/Strategies

D ue to the enormity of the task and the amount of research and analysis that has captivated scholars during the last fifty years in the United States, it appears that feminist work is shifting away from the universal to the particular. There is a consensus that no method works for all.

Tikva Frymer-Kensky, a Hebrew and Jewish scholar, observes, "We are brought to the realization that the Bible contains a fundamental moral flaw: it does not treat all humans as equals. We, in the modern world, are learning that respect for the equality of all human beings and their common dignity is a moral imperative." She concludes that the Bible can no longer be the "arbiter of humanity."[xxxiv] Hence, the development of African Feminist biblical interpretation, Mujerista interpretation, Pakistani, Latin American, Asian Feminist, Korean, Japanese, Womanist, and now, the New Black Female Interpretation has emerged.[xxxv]

Carol Christ is only one of many scholars who have endeavored to argue for the femaleness of the Divine. The Divine is a Sister God, Shekhinah, or a female counterpart to Adonai/God. The Divine is in bondage to patriarchal interpretations. Many researchers have discussed the issue of characterizing or anthropomorphizing the Divine in terms of males only. A male image of the Divine results in the placement of females on a lower rung of society--and there they stay.[xxxvi]

In 1996, Heather A. McKay engaged in research that highlighted the bias of the writers of the New Testament. She studied how the authors of the New Testament books appropriated female characters from the Hebrew Bible. She argues that New Testament writers treated female characters poorly by editing out powerful personality traits, restricting the number of women, and diminishing them by objectifying them. Women become scenery or background for the male characters. "They lose status, force, role, interest, and character." The result is that female readers can become emasculated and lose self-esteem when reading these texts about female characters. [xxxvii] Recent scholarship has also begun to challenge early feminist views that Jesus and his followers were egalitarian. There is a backlash among some interpreters who argue that Christianity was more progressive than Judaism during this time frame.[xxxviii]

Chapter Ten
Disability, Queer, and Transgendered Interpretation

Carol R. Fontaine explores how the academy ignores issues of disability and concludes that scholars have rarely, if at all, explored them in the Bible. She chides, "Any disability or illness which threatens a woman's ability to fulfill her patriarchal purpose strikes at the very heart of her self-esteem, structured as it is by patriarchal expectations, and denies her 'rightful' place within the fabric of society."[xxxix]

In recent days scholars have been studying same-sex relationships and how the topic of gays and lesbians fits into feminist interpretation of the Bible. This new study has been labeled "Queer Biblical Criticism." Jeremy Punt writes, "Queer biblical criticism is [an] 'umbrella term' for the variety of critical approaches encapsulated by it, characterized by their questioning and destabilizing of sexual identities and countering cultural prejudice against sexual minorities."[xl]

For example, Lynne Huffer uses an allegorical feminist-queer interpretation, in discussing the story of Sodom and Gomorrah. Explaining that this text has "justified and sustained centuries of hatred, exclusion, and homophobic violence." She also views misogyny as the very foundation of "queer interpretation." She wonders if the reader can ever escape this historic bigotry. She concludes that even if the reader of the text seeks freedom, she can never find it because the very act of studying the biblical story binds her in some way to the originator, and the very notion of 'other' "scars and traces of the place that is her difference. She cannot escape.[xli]

More recently Rick Talbott, (not exactly Queer criticism) demonstrates by using historical and literary-critical methodologies, that the topic of "eunuch" has been overlooked and misinterpreted by traditional scholars. By juxtaposing a variety of early data about marriage, divorce, castration, and eunuchs in the Roman Empire, he concludes that, "All of Jesus' male disciples were expected to choose to operate under a new definition of being male." He argues that this sets the stage for new relationships between males and females, eliminates gender-bias, and offers people equality instead of kyriarchy.[xlii]

Virginia R. Mollenkott explores issues related to transgendered individuals, people who do not fit the classifications of either a male or a female. She argues that in the New Testament the division of the sexes is often blurred. For example, when studying terms in the New Testament males are included in the image of the "bride of Christ" while women seem to be included in the term "brethren."[xliii]

Chapter Eleven
Marxist Feminist Criticism

Jorunn Økland and Roland Boer, co-edited a volume of papers that explored interpreting the Bible through the lens of Marx and Engels. This collection discusses economic issues and themes that permeate the Bible. Their discoveries encircle the issue of females as property, of exploitative economic value, and how that affects society. For instance, Gale Yee, a scholar of the Hebrew Bible, postulates that intermarriage between the Israelite exiles and locals was a strategic economic decision to acquire land. Jennifer Bird observes that the household code in I Peter silences female voices, controls their sexuality, and subjugates them. A most challenging interpretative approach to the Bible labeled 'Indecent Theology,' in Avaren E. Ipsen's "Solomon and the Two Prostitutes," interprets the story of Solomon and the child with two mothers through the eyes of a prostitute.

In this collection, the most chilling conclusion of all the contributors came from

Jorunn Økland in "Textual Reproduction as Surplus Value: Paul on Pleasing Christ and Spouses, in Light of Simone de Beauvoir." After comparing Paul's works with and Simone de Beauvoir, she writes, "*I am not sure if it is more gratifying to sacrifice your own life in the flesh in order to contribute even more to the surplus value of a greedy university or corporate business than for a greedy church or a greedy Lord....*"[xliv] *Once again we are reminded of how exploited so many of us are, even on the university level.*

Chapter Twelve
Reaction to Feminist Biblical Criticisms

The reaction of some religious groups to the work of feminist biblical scholars is complicated. Mary A. Kassian understands the history of the development of feminist biblical criticism well, but she rejects it. After chronicling a litany of research by feminist scholars including Simone de Beauvoir, Betty Friedan, Rosemary Radford Ruether, Letty Russell, Elizabeth Gould Davis, Elaine Pagels, Letha Scanzoni, Nancy Hardesty, Virginia Mollenkott and more, she rejects all of them and concludes that "feminism and Christianity are anti-thetical." They are an "unholy union." Her argument centers on the fear of damnation that the evangelical church is facing because of the influence of feminism upon it. Her unlikely treatise challenges men and women to follow ancient prescribed roles she says are found in the Bible. The road taken by feminist scholars is too risky.[xlv]

If a researcher believes that the contents of the Bible are inspired by a single Divine voice, the fear of change in interpretative strategies makes sense. After all, the God of the Bible completely annihilates the earth and creates a new one in the Book of Revelation. That fear is profound, especially for women who have born the responsibility of bringing "evil or sin" into the world as suggested by many theologians. After researching the theme of females in the Book of Revelation, I wonder, "Could the annihilation of the earth in Revelation 20 represent the ultimate and final alienation/annihilation of Mother Earth, of woman?"[xlvi]

Hector Avalos has come to the same conclusion regarding Biblical studies. Avalos agrees with many of the tenets of feminist biblical interpretation but he argues that, "Biblical Studies as we know it should end." And to a large extent this has always been the goal of feminists who are attempting to change the interpretation landscape to include diverse approaches to the Bible. How can *ancient and dated interpretative approaches* to interpretation continue when they disenfranchise so many people?[xlvii]

Chapter Thirteen
Final Thoughts and the Future

Feminist Biblical Interpretation is in a tremendous growth pattern. Surely the terms and trajectories will continue to change. There is already pressure to rename it "Gender" interpretation. Elisabeth Schüssler Fiorenza, in "The Power of the Word: Charting Critical Global Feminist Biblical Studies," suggests that, "The 'new field' of critical feminist interpretation is positioned in-between globalization and localization, universality and particularity, isolationism and networking, disinterested academy and social movement, difference and differences, modernism and postmodernism." [xlviii]

One could only hope that her analysis is correct. My research suggests that most feminist biblical research is becoming more specialized, nationalistic, personal, and particular. This trend as noted above has caused dissension, and will probably not facilitate consensus on feminist issues and interpretations.

After all of the research on the topic of feminist biblical interpretation, it is glaringly apparent that there are many people within diverse religious communities who do not want to abandon the androcentric interpretations of the traditions encased in the Bible. It has a psychic hold on them. In spite of the vociferous critiques and discoveries of misogynistic, imperialistic, and violent tendencies in many biblical writings and the communities it produced, they continue to hold the Bible close to their hearts even though it "stings" them. A. I. Waskow, in *God Wrestling* would agree, "We do not simply accept the traditions, but we do not reject it either. We wrestle with it: fighting it and making love to it at the same time."[xlix]

The Bible is a historic collection of thoughts that has shaped countries and peoples for millennia. Communities have centered their faith activities in the Bible, brought unlikely people together, and serviced many needy people in spite of its misogyny, advocacy of male supremacy, and war-like tendencies. Communities like this provide havens and extended families for people. For some, to give up the study and research of the Bible may result in losing those friends or a haven. The flight of some Protestants away from feminist biblical traditions is understandable because they believe it essentially erodes their belief-system about order in society and community life. They cannot risk the loss even if it means redeeming oppressed females and others who constitute more than half of their congregations.

Feminists also desire control of the interpretation of the text to disseminate their truth, because it often legitimates an alternate power structure and serves to control myth. And, yes, they want more power in their lives and more control over the people who oppress, marginalize, and exploit them. But perhaps they could also open their research and hearts to others who also suffer in much the same way.

While it is not always a positive experience to meditate on the image of sacrifice, it is a useful metaphor when we look into the future of feminist biblical interpretation. Could people who study the Bible begin to be less greedy for retribution and vindication? Could they sacrifice some of the power they so crave on behalf of kindness, generosity, and appreciation of the plights and problems of others? Could they be less vengeful toward males and their scholarship? Could they stop searching for the "Truth" and recognize that there are many paths and many truths, and allow others to follow their own paths or ways without attacking them?

When I was a professor in a state university in the heartland of the United States I was overwhelmed daily by the lack of exposure by administrators, faculty, students, and staff to feminist theory and goals of equity. They not only ignored it, they demonstrated hostility toward it. It upsets the order of things for them. Certainly a state university is not a community of faith, but a large percentage of the people who work at this university and attend classes, claim homes in traditional religions with foundations in the Bible. There is a decided disconnect between feminist theory and methodology, progress toward equity, and the realities of life, daily politics, and survival.

While we may be publishing new ideas about how we should interpret the Bible differently, or discovering people in the past who have shared the same dream, or how culture should change, or how political power should be shared, on a very basic level the average person does not understand shared power, and many have an unimpeachable belief in male supremacy that systematically excludes those who would challenge it.

Significant change may have come to some religious communities but not to society as a whole in my view. Naomi Goldenberg threatened that feminism would be the end of traditional religions when the male God would be eliminated in her book *The Changing of the Gods* in 1979. "God is going to change.... We women are going to bring and end to God.... We will change the world so much that He won't fit in anymore."[xlx] Naomi Goldenberg's prophecies failed to materialize. Little has changed. Perhaps her prophecies will come true ... someday.

Notes

[11] For example: Ron Cameron, *The Other Gospels. Noncanonical Gospel Texts*. Philadelphia: Westminster Press, 1982.

[2] Elizabeth Fox-Genovese, "For Feminist Interpretation," *Union Seminary Quarterly Review* 35, 2&3, 1979-1980; p. 8

[3] Ibid, p. 6

[4] Ibid, p. 14

[5] Pamela Milne, "No Promised Land: Rejecting the Authority of the Bible," in   *Feminist Approaches to the Bible. Symposium at the Smithsonian Institution*, September 24, 1994. Washington, Biblical Archaeology   ociety, 1995, p. 69.

[6] T. Drorah Setel, "Feminist Insights and the Question of Method," in Adela Yarbro Collins, *Feminist Perspectives on Biblical Scholarship* Society of Biblical Literature, 1996, p. 39

[7] Elisabeth Schüssler Fiorenza, *The Power of the Word: Scripture and Rhetoric of Empire*. Minneapolis: Fortress Press, 2007, p. 254.

[8] Elisabeth Schüssler Fiorenza *Wisdom Ways. Introducing Feminist Biblical Interpretation*. Maryknoll: Orbis, 2001, p. 6

[9] Richard Soulen and R. Kendall Soulen, *Handbook of Biblical Criticism. Third Edition* Louisville, Kentucky: Westminster John Knox, 2001, p. 58.

[10] Joanne Carlson Brown and Rebecca Parker, "For God so Loved the World?" in Joanne Carlson Brown and Carole R. Bohn, editors, *Christianity, Patriarchy, and Abuse: A Feminist Critique* Cleveland, Ohio: The Pilgrim Press, 1989, p. 9. See also: Phyllis Trible, *Texts of Terror. Literary Feminist Readings of Biblical Narratives Philadelphia*: Fortress Press, 1984.

[11] Leonard Swidler, "Jesus Was a Feminist," *Catholic World* (January 1971, Vol. 212), pp. 177-183.

[12] For example: David M. Scholer, "Feminist Hermeneutics and Evangelical Biblical Interpretation," *Journal of Evangelical Theological Studies* (30/4 December 1987) 407-420.

[13] My apologies for methodologies that were not included.

[xiv] Friedrich W. Nietzsche, *Beyond Good and Evil* Trans. Helen Zimmer Buffalo, New York: Prometheus Books, 1989, p. 97.

[xv] Paul D. Hanson, *The Dawn of Apocalyptic Eschatology The Historical and Sociological Roots of Jewish Apocalyptic* (Minneapolis: Fortress, 1979.

[xvi] See Christiana de Groot and Marion Ann Taylor, editors. *Recovering Nineteenth Century Women Interpreters of the Bible.* Atlanta: Society of Biblical Literature, 2007.

[xvii] Carol Christ, Editor, *Womanspirit Rising. A Feminist Reader in Religion* San Francisco: Harper-Collins, 1979 and 1992.

[xviii] Letty M. Russell, editor. *Feminist Interpreters of the Bible* (Philadelphia: Westminster Press, 1985 , p. 11. A good summary of the history of feminist biblical criticism may be found: Carolyn De Swarte Gifford, "American Women and the Bible: The Nature of Woman as a Hermeneutical Issue," in Adela Yarbro Collins, editor, *Feminist Perspectives on Biblical Scholarship* Chico: Scholars Press, 1985, pp. 11-34.

[xix] Patrick M. Arnold, *Wildmen, Warriors, and Kings: Masculine Spirituality and the Bible* New York: Crossroads, 1991, pp. 51-63.

[xx] Elizabeth Cady Stanton, editor of *The Woman"s Bible* New York: European Publishing Company, 1898. Reprint Seattle, Washington: Coalition   Task Force on Women and Religion, 1974.

[xxi] Phyllis Trible, "Depatriarchalizing in Biblical Perspective," in Elizabeth Koltun *The Jewish Woman. New Perspectives.* New York: Schocken Books, 1976, pp. 217, 227, 234.

[xxii] Laura Swan. *The Forgotten Desert Mothers. Sayings, Lives, and Stories of Early Christian Women,* New York: Paulist Press, 2001, p. 37.

[xxiii] Ibid, p. 41.

[xxiv] Alcun Blamires, *Woman Defamed and Woman Defended. An Anthology of Medieval Texts* Oxford: Oxford University Press, 1992, p. 233.

[xxv] See unpublished presentations by Marla J. Selvidge "Florence and Imperial Christianity," and "The Art and Architecture of Florence," summer of 2010, Royal Caribbean Cruise Lines.

[xxvi] Marla J. Selvidge, *Notorious Voices. Feminist Biblical Interpretation 1500-1920* New York: Continuum, 1996, p. 208.

xxvii Ibid., p. 175.

xxviii Charlotte Perkins Gilman, *Herland*, New York: Pantheon Books, 1979 Early edition 1915). A full copy may be found on-line at: http://etext.virginia.edu/toc/modeng/public/GilHerl.html

xxix Matilda Joslyn Gage, *Woman, Church and State: A Historical Account of the Status Woman through the Christian Ages: with Reminiscences of the Matriarchate.* Annette K. Baxter and Leon Stein, eds. New York: The Truth Seeker Company, 1900. Reprint: Arno Press, 1972. See also: Matilda Joslyn Gage, *Woman, Church, and the State. The Original Expose of Male Collaboration Against the Female* Sex, Watertown, MA: Persephone Press, 1980 (Original 1893).

xxx Mary Daly, *The Church and the Second Sex* Boston: Beacon Press, 1968; Simone de Beauvoir, *The Second Sex*, 1949.

xxxi Emerson B. Powery, "'Rise Up, Ye Women': Harriet Jacobs and the Bible," *Postscripts* 5.2, 2011, 171-184.

xxxii Katharine C. Bushnell, *God"s Word to Women. One Hundred Bible Studies on Woman"s Place in the Divine Economy* Piedmont, California: Published via reprint, ed. Ray Munson, Box 52, North Collins, N.Y.,   1976, 1921. See # 616, 151, 152. For a full copy see: http://www.godswordtowomen.org/gwtw.htm

xxxiii Lee Anna Starr, *The Bible Status of Woman*, New York: Fleming H. Revell, 1926. Paragraphs #341 and #176.

xxxiv Tikva Frymer-Kensky, "The Bible and Women"s Studies," in Lynn Davidman and   Shelly Tenenbaum, editors, *Feminist Perspectives on Jewish Studies* New Haven: Yale University Press, 1994, p.18

xxxvSee R. S. Sugirtharajah, Voices from the Margin. *Interpreting the Bible in the Third World* Maryknoll: Orbis, 1991.

xxxvi Carol Christ, "Women"s Liberation and the Liberation of God: An Essay in Story Theology," in Elizabeth Koltun, *The Jewish Woman. New Perspectives.* New York: Schocken Books, 1976, p. 13.

xxxvii Heather A. McKay, "'Only a Remnant of Them Shall be S aved.'" Women from the Hebrew Bible in New Testament Narratives," in Athalya Brenner, *A Feminist Companion to the Hebrew Bible in the New Testament* Sheffield Academic Press: England, 1993. pp. 59, 61.

xxxviii Mary Ann Beavis, "Christian Origins, Egalitarianism, and Utopia," in *Journal of Feminist Studies in Religions* 2, 23 (2007), pp. 27-49.

xxxix Carol R. Fontaine, "Disabilities and Illness in the Bible: A Feminist Perspective," in Athalya Brenner, *A Feminist Companion to the Hebrew Bible in the New Testament* Sheffield Academic Press: England, 1993. pp. 291.

xl Jeremy Punt, "Intersections of Queer Theory and Postcolonial Theory, and Hermeneutical Spinoffs," *The Bible and Critical Theory*, 4(2, 2008): 24:1

xli Lynn Huff, "There is no Gomorrah. Narrative Ethics in Feminist and Queer Theory." *Differences. A Journal of Feminist Cultural Studies* 12.3 (2001): pp. 2, 22.

xlii Rick, Talbott, "Imaging the Matthean Eunuch Community. Kyriarchy on the Chopping Block," *Journal of Feminist Studies in Religion* 22(1,2006): p. 40.

xliii Virginia R. Mollenkot, *Omnigender. A Trans-religious Approach* (Cleveland: The Pilgrim Press, 2007) 126-129. See also books on heterosexism.)

xliv Roland Boer, and Jorunn Økland, *Marxist Feminist Criticism of the Bible. Bible in the Modern World* 14 Sheffield: Sheffield Phoenix, 2008, p. 202.

xlv Mary A. Kassian, *The Feminist Gospel. The Movement to Unite Feminism with the Church.* Wheaton, Crossway Books, 1992, pp. 239, 253.

xlvi Marla J. Selvidge, "Reflections on Violence and Pornography: Misogyny in the Apocalypse and Ancient Hebrew Prophecy," in Athalya Brenner, *A Feminist Companion to the Hebrew Bible in the New Testament* Sheffield, England: Sheffield Academic Press, 1996, p. 285.

xlvii Hector Avalos, *The End of Biblical Studies.* New York: Prometheus Books, 2007, p. 339.

xlviii Elisabeth Schüssler Fiorenza, "The Power of the Word: Charting Critical Global Feminist Biblical Studies," in Kathleen O'Brien Wicker, Althea Spencer Miller, and Musa W. Dube, editors. *Feminist New Testament Studies. Global and Future Perspectives,* New York: Palgrave, 2005, p. 54

xlix A. I. Waskow, *God Wrestling* New York: Schocken, 1978, p. 11

xlx Naomi Goldenberg, *The Changing of the Gods. Feminism and the End of Traditional Religions* Boston: Beacon Press, 1979 p. 3.

About the Authoress

Marla J. Selvidge, Ph.D. retired as Professor and Director of the Center for Religious Studies at the University of Central Missouri. She founded the Center in 1990 and directed its growth, developing thirty courses, as well as an academic major and minor, plus scores of public programs. Having published numerous academic books and articles, her most recent work is *Life Everlasting and the Twelve Mile Blues*, a personal memoir and research on Kentucky. Hailing from Roseville, Michigan, she has spent most of her career teaching in colleges and universities. Her Ph.D. is from Saint Louis University and the M.A. was awarded at Wheaton Graduate School. She resides with her husband, Thomas C. Hemling, Ph.D. a Global Research Director, and Princess Twinkers, in a suburb of Kansas City, Missouri. Together for over thirty years, they have traveled to at least sixty countries and plan to keep on traveling. For correspondence with Dr. Marla you can email her at selvidge@ucmo.edu

www.ingramcontent.com/pod-product-compliance
Lightning Source LLC
Chambersburg PA
CBHW070541030426
42337CB00016B/2294